T0193171

The Greatest Miracle of All

A story accompanied by illustrations embedded in photographs of biblical sites from the Holy Land

THE STORY OF JESUS

By Aia Laser

Illustrated by Hanan Kaminski

Photographed by Amiram Jablonovsky

Dedicated to the proposition that war is not an inevitable, and through education, understanding and social interaction, peace is achievable and sustainable in our lifetime…

Produced by Aia Laser
Graphics by Yana Tilman

To order additional copies of this book, contact:
Xlibris
844-714-8691
www.Xlibris.com
Orders@Xlibris.com

Library of Congress Control Number: 2002096271
ISBN: Softcover978-1-4010-8527-8

Print information available on the last page

Rev. date: 02/05/2024

The Greatest Miracle of All

A story accompanied by illustrations embedded in photographs of biblical sites from the Holy Land

THE STORY OF JESUS

By Aia Laser

Illustrated by Hanan Kaminski

Photographed by Amiram Jablonovsky

It all began 2,000 years ago, in the city of Nazareth. There lived a young virgin named Mary.

One day, the angel Gabriel came down from the sky to tell Mary that she would become the mother of God's child.

"Your son will be the savior of the world, and his name will be Jesus," said Gabriel to Mary's great surprise.

Then he disappeared back into the sky.

Nazareth. Basilica of the Annunciation.

Nine months later, the baby Jesus was born in the city of Bethlehem.

That night, the angels danced in the sky and sang happy songs to the newborn child.

Even the shepherds came from the fields to greet the baby Jesus and everyone was thrilled.
It was exciting!
But an even greater miracle was coming.

Bethlehem. Cave of the Nativity. On the silver star beneath the altar these words have been carved in Latin:
"Here Jesus Christ was born of the Virgin Mary"

Baby Jesus grew into a fine boy.

Together with Mary's husband, Joseph, he worked as a carpenter.

Yet Jesus was a very special boy. He was always aware of other people's needs and gave comfort to the poor and the weak.

No wonder many people loved Jesus and followed him everywhere.
He was perfect!

Nazareth. Church of St. Joseph.

Years passed, and when Jesus became a man, he went with his disciples from town to town.

He used his power to perform great miracles that only God could do.

Jesus made lame people walk, blind people see and mute people sing.

He even brought dead people back to life!

Capernaum.

But there were other miracles too.

One day, five thousand people gathered to hear Jesus speak but as the hour turned late they became very hungry and weak.

So Jesus took five loaves of bread and two fish, and turned them into enough food for everyone to eat!

Tabgha. Church of the Multiplication of the Loaves and Fishes.

For three years, there was one miracle after another. But the greatest miracle of all was still about to happen.

Then, the time had come for Jesus and his disciples to go to Jerusalem. On their way, Jesus found a quiet place and revealed to them the secret he had always kept.
"I will be killed in Jerusalem," Jesus said, "but on the third day I will come back to life."

The disciples looked at each other. It was hard for them to believe that something could happen to Jesus, their beloved teacher.

Tiberias. Area of Galilee.

Jerusalem. Mount of Olives.

As Jesus and his disciples entered Jerusalem, they found themselves in the middle of a big celebration. Jesus rode a little donkey, while people threw their cloaks along his way and cheered, "Hosanna! Blessed is he who comes in the name of the Lord!"

On the side of the road, children danced and greeted Jesus with palm branches in their hands.

Jerusalem. The Cenacle - Last Supper room.

A few days later, Jesus joined his disciples for dinner. But his heart was heavy. He knew that soon it would all come to an end.

"Drink the wine and eat the bread," said Jesus. "Do this in remembrance of me."

The disciples didn't understand what Jesus meant. The thought of losing him was too much for them to bear.

Jesus felt sad. Now, more than ever, he needed to talk with God. He left the room and prayed in the garden outside.

"Father, I do not want to die," Jesus said, "but if that is what you want, I accept it with all my heart." Jesus knew that he must die. If he didn't, the people would never be forgiven for their sins.

Suddenly, a large crowd of angry people carrying swords and clubs came into the garden. They were looking for Jesus.

Jerusalem. Garden of Gethsemane.

The people arrested Jesus and took him to be tried in the high priest's house.

But they were not interested in the truth.

"This man claims to be the Son of God! He should die!" they shouted, and they beat Jesus throughout the night.

Jerusalem. The ancient pathway with steps descending from the neighborhood of the Cenacle to the Kidron Valley.

But Jesus was not afraid and he did not try to run away. He knew that God was on his side, so he suffered it all with great fortitude.

Jerusalem. "The Dungeon" - located inside the Church of St. Peter in Gallicantu.

The next morning, Jesus was handed over to Pontius Pilate, the Roman governor.

"I find nothing wrong with this man," said Pilate, but the people's hearts were still full of hate.

"Crucify him! Crucify him!" the angry people yelled, "we want him dead!"

Jesus heard everything they said, but he was not afraid. His heart was so good and pure that he loved them all, despite their terrible words.

Jerusalem. Arch of the "Ecce Homo", where the Roman trial took place.

The people screamed and yelled until Pilate finally said, "If you want him dead, do it yourselves."

Then the soldiers hit Jesus and mocked him. They put a crown of thorns on his head and made him carry a heavy wooden cross up a hill called Golgotha.

Many people followed Jesus on his last journey. Some of them cried and felt very sad, for they knew that Jesus was, indeed, the beloved Son of God.

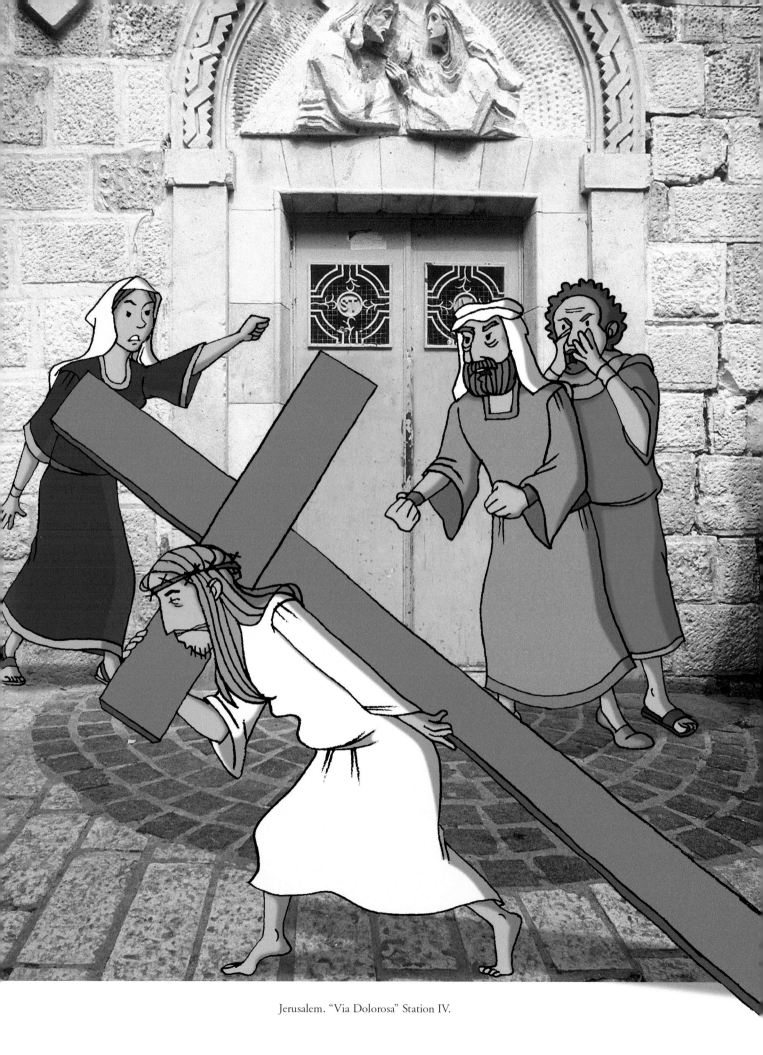

Jerusalem. "Via Dolorosa" Station IV.

The soldiers nailed the hands and feet of Jesus to the cross and left him there to die.

"Father, forgive them," Jesus prayed as he tried to overcome his pain, "they do not know what they are doing."

Jesus remained on the cross for many hours.
Then, at the ninth hour, the whole earth shook, the rocks split wide and darkness filled the sky.

"It is finished!" Jesus cried.
Then he bowed down his head and died.

Jerusalem. The present entrance to the Basilica of the Holy Sepulchre.

Jesus' body was taken down from the cross.

A man placed the body in a tomb and rolled a heavy stone over the entrance.

The disciples, who saw what had happened, couldn't stop crying. Their hearts were broken. They couldn't understand why Jesus – the man who loved the whole world – had to die.

Do you know why?

Jerusalem. The tomb of Jesus inside the Basilica of the Holy Sepulchre. The site of Jesus' burial and Resurrection.

Early on the first Easter morning, however, everything changed.

Three women who made up spices for after Sabbath day came near the tomb and noticed that the stone was rolled away from the entrance.

They slowly entered the tomb and found, to their surprise, that it was empty!

Suddenly they saw an angel from heaven heading towards them.

"Why is he here," the women wondered, "and where is Jesus?"

"The Lord Jesus is no longer here," the angel said, "he is risen!"

"He's alive! Jesus is alive! It's the greatest miracle of all!" the women shouted as tears of joy rolled down their faces.

Very soon the word was spread – "The Lord Jesus is no longer dead! He rose from the grave!"

Jerusalem, Basilica of the Holy Sepulchre. The exterior of the shrine built over Jesus' tomb.

When the disciples heard the news they did not know whether to believe it or not. Then suddenly, Jesus was standing near them.

The disciples were not sure if it was really him or just a dream. So they touched Jesus' hands and side and realized that he was, indeed, alive!

They were so excited!

A few days later, Jesus appeared to them again, near the Sea of Galilee. Together they ate fish and bread, in remembrance of the beautiful days that they had spent.

Tabgha, on the Lake of Gennesaret. Church of St. Peter.

Then it was time for Jesus to go back to heaven. He blessed his disciples and rose up into the sky until a cloud hid him from sight.

Jesus loved the world, and now the world loves him back.
Let us continue his work on earth.

Together, we can make this world a better place to live, for we all have something special to give.
Let us do it, for you and for me.
It's the only way to be.

Printed in the United States
by Baker & Taylor Publisher Services